Power Training

D0770515

The Body Coach Series

Power Training

Build your most powerful body ever

with Australia's Body Coach®

Paul Collins

Meyer & Meyer Sports

British Library Cataloguing in Publication Data
A catalogue record for this book is available from the British Library

Paul Collins
Power Training
Maidenhead: Meyer & Meyer Sport (UK) Ltd., 2008
ISBN 978-1-84126-233-8

© 2008 by by Paul Collins (text & photos)
and Meyer & Meyer Sport (UK) Ltd. (Layout)
Aachen, Adelaide, Auckland, Budapest, Graz, Indianapolis, Johannesburg,
Maidenhead, New York, Olten (CH), Singapore, Toronto
Member of the World
Sport Publishers' Association (WSPA)
www.w-s-p-a.org

Printed and bound by: B.O.S.S Druck und Medien GmbH, Germany
ISBN 978-1-84126-233-8
E-Mail: verlag@m-m-sports.com
www.m-m-sports.com

Sept 2010

Introduction

Welcome!

I'm The Body Coach®, Paul Collins, your exclusive personal coach here to guide and motivate towards developing your most powerful body ever using your own body weight. A major breakthrough in exercising, Power Training provides practical hands-on training drills for helping improve athletic performance. What's more, Power Training is an excellent way for conditioned athletes to increase and develop their jumping, sprinting and explosive power. So for this reason, to be effective 100% focus is required.

For many years coaches and athletes have sought to improve power, a combination of speed and strength, in order to enhance performance. As a result, Power Training is designed as an educational tool to assist in the development of training programs that aim to keep athletes fit, strong and powerful all year round. The athletes that will benefit most from power training are those that require speed-strength – the ability to exert maximal forces during high speed movements whilst maintaining perfect technique.

The exercises prescribed are the exact ones used by Olympic and World Class athletes in a number of sports as part of their training programs. Packed with more than 80 Power Training Drills, Tests and Training Routines over nine chapters you now have the ultimate range of exercises available to you for improving your power and athletic performance.

I look forward to working with you!

Paul Collins

The Body Coach

About the Author

Paul Collins is an award-winning personal trainer in Australia, a prolific author on fitness and weight loss topics and General Manager of the Australian Academy of Sport and Fitness, an International College in Sydney, Australia specifically for overseas students wishing to study and obtain fitness and personal training qualifications. Each year Paul inspires thousands of people through appearances on TV, radio and print media and seminars.

Coaching since age 14, Paul has personally trained world-class athletes and teams in a variety of sports, e.g., athletics, rugby, soccer, squash, tennis and many others including members of the Australian Olympic Swimming Team. He is also a key presenter to the Australian Track and Field Coaching Association, Australia Swimming Coaches and Teachers Association, NSW Squash Academy and the Australian Fitness Industry. Paul is an outstanding athlete is his own right, having played grade level in the National Rugby League. He is also a former Australian Budokan Karate Champion, A-grade Squash Player and NSW Masters Athletics Track & Field State Champion.

As a leader in the field of personal fitness and weight loss, Paul has successfully combined a sports fitness background with a Bachelor of Physical Education Degree and international certification as a strength and conditioning coach and personal trainer. As designer of *The Body Coach* book series, exercise products and educational programs, Paul travels internationally to present a highly entertaining series of corporate health & well-being seminars and exclusive five-star personal training for VIPs.

For more details visit: www.thebodycoach.com

Contents

Acknowledgements

I would like to thank the following people in the development of this book: Photographers Leon Collins, Linda Collins and Amanda Cartaar; My parents and family for involving me in an active sporting life; Fitness gurus Rob Rowland Smith, Clayton Kearney, Ron Palmer; Senseis Wayne MacDonald, Donna Sutor and Daniel Spice of Karate Budokan International and Life Coach Howard Wells who have helped guide and inspire my journey in life.

Note: Body Coach®, The Body Coach®, Fastfeet®, Quickfeet®, Posturefit®, Speedhoop®, Spinal Unloading Block®; Collins-Technique™, Rebound Medicine Ball™, 3B's Principle™ and Australia's Personal Trainer™ are all trademarks of Paul Collins.

Chapter 1

Power Plyometric Training

For decades athletes and coaches have sought to improve power, a combination of speed and strength, in order to enhance athletic and sports performance. *Power Training* is designed to bring "attention to detail" of all power exercises and their associated movement patterns using ones own body weight and resistance such as a medicine ball. The main goal of all power exercises is focusing on quality of movement with each exercise, so exercises are performed with good technique and without fatigue.

Running at high speed is a powerful movement pattern. An efficient running style developed through regular practice of running technique and specific power drills enables the body to adapt with synergistic fluency between muscle groups. Hence, a fast athlete who is able to maintain excellent body position and running technique over the full distance of the sprint is one of the outcomes of proper power training. In addition, learning specific power drills involving jumping, hopping and bounding will assist with body awareness and motor coordination allowing muscles to fire quicker and more efficiently.

What are Plyometrics?

Plyometrics are a form of exercise designed to produce the greatest strength gains in as short a time as possible. Running, jumping, hopping, bounding and skipping, with landings, are all forms of plyometric movement patterns performed in sports from a young age right up to Olympic level competition. The phrase power using one's body weight is often referred to as Plyometrics – developed in Eastern Europe for Olympic competitors. The words 'plyo' and 'metrics' are Latin for "measurable increases."

A plyometric exercise is an exercise in which an **eccentric** muscle contraction is quickly followed by a **concentric** muscle contraction. In other words, when a muscle is rapidly contracted and lengthened, and then immediately followed with a further contraction and shortening, this is referred to as a plyometric movement pattern. An **eccentric** muscle contraction occurs when your muscle contracts and lengthens at the same time, where as a **concentric** muscle contraction occurs when your muscle contracts and shortens at the same time. This process of contract-lengthen, contract-shorten is often referred to as the **stretch shortening cycle (SSC)**.

Plyometrics utilize the forces of gravity to store potential energy in the muscles, and then quickly turn this stored energy into kinetic energy. For example, when a person jumps off a step, lands on the ground with both feet and then jumps forwards – all in one swift movement – this is referred to as a plyometric movement. When you jump off the step and land on the ground, the muscles in your legs contract eccentrically to slow your body down. Then, when you jump forward your muscles contract concentrically to spring you off the ground.

The in-depth jump (box jump) is a specific plyometric exercise example; the athlete steps off the box and lands, legs coiled (potential energy is stored), then quickly leaps to the next box (kinetic energy is utilized). The natural elastic properties of the muscle serve as excellent storehouses for the energy. To gain the maximum benefits of plyometrics it is important to note that the stored energy must be immediately used in an opposite direction.

In sprints and jumps it is now recognized that athletes who spend the least amount of time on the ground generally display the greatest jumping performances. Based on this observation it is assumed that athletes' muscles must also be strong eccentrically in order to withstand the high mechanical forces placed on the body. Hence, training the muscles eccentrically should enable athletes to overcome the eccentric loading quickly to concentrically contracting immediately, propelling the body in the desired direction. This allows the athlete to exploit the energy stored in the muscle during the eccentric stretch phase. Therefore, by increasing the amount of tension the athlete can generate during the eccentric contraction and by improving the reactive ability of the muscles in switching from eccentric to concentric work, possible improvements in jump performance can be made.

THE BODY COACH

However, in order for improvements to be made, proper power progressions must exist.

Muscle Mechanism

The maximum force that a muscle can develop is attained during a rapid eccentric contraction. However, it should be realized that muscles seldom perform one type of contraction in isolation during athletic movements. When a concentric contraction occurs immediately following an eccentric contraction, then the force generated can be dramatically increased.

If a muscle is stretched, much of the energy required to stretch it is lost as heat, but some of this energy can be stored by the elastic components of the muscle. This stored energy is available to the muscle only during a subsequent contraction. It is important to realize that this energy boost is lost if the eccentric contraction is not followed immediately by a concentric effort. To express this greater force the muscle must contract within the shortest time possible. Once again, this whole process is called the Stretch Shortening Cycle (SSC) and is the underlying mechanism of plyometric training. Hence, plyometric training should progress gradually from lower intensity to higher intensity drills, especially for individuals who lack a significant strength training background.

Goal of Power Development

The goal of any power training program should therefore gradually progress each individual athlete through a series of low- to medium-level power exercises that teach the basic fundamentals of each movement pattern, namely jumping and landing, to ensure an effective strength base is acquired before progressing to more dynamic high intensity drills. What many athletes need to first understand is how important the motor efficiency is in each power movement. By this I refer to correct body posture and biomechanical efficiency when performing a drill or movement pattern individually or as part of a sequence over an extended period of time.

Learning how to correctly perform each exercise at a low to moderate intensity first, allows the body, its muscles, joints, tendons and ligaments together with the Central Nervous System (CNS) to adapt successfully to these demands. This approach enables the athlete to focus on maintaining perfect body position and technique as a priority when performing any power exercise. Too great a load can reduce the speed and quality of movement negating the effects of plyometrics. Therefore, power exercises generally start as short intense bursts of energy that focus on maintaining good posture, technique and motor coordination. As the movement is mastered then the intensity levels are increased. But no matter what your current level of fitness, every participant needs to start from the very beginning with low intensity exercises and progress through these over a minimum preparation period of 4-6 weeks before attempting medium to high intensity exercises. This is the core ingredient to successful power development.

Understanding Strength and Power

There are a number of differences to conventional training that need to be outlined when first describing power training. The first relates to the difference between strength and power training in this instance. In a training environment, strength exercises are generally performed until physiological (muscle) fatigue occurs between 8-10 repetitions when performing an exercise (for example: push-ups or bench press). In this instance, power exercises being performed using one's body weight as the resistance in a fast movement pattern can quite often cause minimal physiological fatigue, yet higher nervous system fatigue and stress on the joints. This is where the first problem arises: athletes used to physiological fatigue in strength training may quite often transfer a similar approach towards power training, when the opposite is required. The major point is that all power exercises need to be performed in a fresh state with adequate recovery time between exercises to ensure that quality of each exercise, including posture and body mechanics, are maintained. Hence, many exercises may look easy to perform, but don't be fooled as the stress placed on the muscle, joints, ligaments and tendons when jumping and landing differs dramatically. And, the risk of injury is high if not performed properly and under the guidance of a qualified coach.

Because of a high level of muscle imbalance amongst athletes and weak core-muscles (abdominal and lower back region), the importance of correct technique in a power training program is vital. A weak or imbalanced body places stressors on particular muscle groups and joints around the body that can become tight or chronically inflamed over a period of time, which is hard to reverse. Like any form of training a proper warm-up, cool down and stretching period plays an important role. Core-strengthening is vital. And because of the demanding nature of the exercises additional sports massage and regular physiotherapy adjustments may be necessary to keep muscles pliable.

Strength Base

Conventional wisdom dictates that certain prerequisite levels of strength as well as strength training experience are recommended to safely perform power plyometric exercises. The purpose of plyometrics is to improve the athlete's capacity to apply more force more rapidly. Logically then, the greater the athlete's ability to generate maximal force or strength to begin with, the more of it can be converted into sport-specific power. Criteria such as male athletes being able to squat at least 1 to 1.5 times their body weight (0.50–0.75 for female athletes) are quite high in many cases. Basic strength is important in order to forcefully contract the muscles concentrically while also withstanding the increased forces placed on the body, particularly the back, hips, knees, and ankles. For youth, these criteria for maximal strength may be of less significance, as most are unrealistic, especially considering the relatively low body weight. In my experience, youth should only perform low intensity power exercises focusing on developing balance, stabilization, motor coordination and core strength as a prerequisite with a focus on mastering movement technique – jumping, landing, squat and lunge. Either way, all power plyometric exercises should always be performed under the guidance and supervision of a qualified coach.

Eccentric strength is a limiting factor in the more complex plyometric exercises. Without sufficient levels of eccentric strength, the athlete will not be able to switch from eccentric to concentric strength quickly, which reduces the duration of the ground contact phase. Improving eccentric strength should also be emphasized prior to plyometric training through strength exercises such as squats and lunges for the lower body and push-ups and chin-ups for the upper body. Performing tests such as static stands and single leg squats are good tests of the stabilizing strength of the hips, torso, ankle and foot. Testing of posture, balance, stability, flexibility and motor coordination as well fitness levels is a prerequisite prior to participation in power training.

Intensity Levels of Power Exercises

Power exercises vary in both complexity and intensity and should be taught in a progressive manner that suits the participant's skill and ability level. Plyometrics are a form of progressive resistance exercise and thus, must follow the principles of progressive overload. Progressive overload is a systematic increase in frequency, volume, and intensity by various combinations of exercises. Keep in mind that when one or two of these variables are increased, one or both of the other variables may decrease. Generally, as intensity increases volume will decrease. Intensity levels for plyometric exercises have been classified as:

- Low intensity
- Medium intensity
- High intensity or Shock (elite athletes only)

Skipping exercises are classed as low intensity, while reactive drop jumps from a platform are the highest intensity. Low intensity exercises are the first to be introduced to a beginner. Exercises classified as low intensity are typically in-place jumps. These are mainly performed on two legs and, when compared to higher intensity exercises, the reaction phase is longer. These are the most simple of all plyometric exercises.

Intermediate level exercises are classified as medium intensity. Medium intensity exercises are classified by short responses. They can be performed with either double or single leg movements. Moderate intensity exercises include tucks, hops, and bounds. The reaction phase becomes faster as intensity increases. High intensity exercises should only be performed by advanced athletes who have first displayed proficiency in the low and medium intensity exercises. Single leg exercises are performed more often than double leg movements. Responses are also longer for high intensity exercises. High intensity exercises can include lateral, diagonal, and incline movements. They may also include barriers. The reaction phase during high intensity exercises should be very rapid.

High intensity shock exercises are at the end of the plyometric stress continuum. These are also known as depth jumps. These are the most complex of the plyometric exercises. Depth jumps involve falls or jumps from a predetermined height and upon landing, immediately jumping upward or forward. Depth jumping demands dynamic strength to withstand the forces upon landing, but also develops the reactive ability of the muscle to switch from eccentric work to concentric work rapidly. Many of the injuries that occur from plyometric training result from attempting to perform these exercises without properly progressing through low, medium, and high intensity level exercises first over an extended period of training. It is important to remember that as intensity increases, power plyometric volume must decrease. All of these exercises must be taught progressively in order to maximize performance and should only be performed after proper progressions have been met as depth jumps are of the highest intensity.

Preconditions

Prior to participating in power training each athlete must first establish a speed and resistance training base. Hence, several criteria need to be met before instituting a power plyometric training program.

Fitness Level

The strength and conditioning level of the athlete must be considered prior to performing plyometrics. If the athlete does not possess sufficient muscular strength or sufficient fitness levels, injury or overtraining may result. Any athlete wanting to perform power exercises should first be screened by a physiotherapist to ensure musculoskeletal efficiency and balance. Various stretching, core-strengthening and stability exercises may also be provided by the physiotherapist to ensure muscle efficiency. Athletes must also gain medical clearance by a doctor before starting any new exercise or program. Because of the demands of power training each athlete needs to implement a body management program that incorporates an effective warm-up and cooldown period, stretching routine and physiotherapy and massage plan. This can be implemented under the guidance of a certified strength and conditioning coach who will demonstrate and observe each athlete's performance.

Physical Maturity of the Athlete

Physical maturity is usually determined by an athlete's ability to perform a range of strength, fitness, flexibility and motor coordination tests favorably. In some instances, it is recommended that an athlete be able to squat 1.5 to 2.5 their own body weight – a minimum standard for high-intensity shock oriented plyometrics. For the upper body, it is recommended that athletes be able to bench press 1 to 1.5 times their own body weight. The ability to perform 40 straight push-ups without loss of form and five continuous clap push-ups are also exercises for testing the physical maturity of the athlete.

Athlete Coachability

Coachability refers to the athlete being able to respond in a positive fashion to instructions and criticism. If not, plyometric training should be delayed to prevent injury, overtraining, or undertraining. If the athlete will not respond to coaching direction they often will not perform the movements properly. This can result in poor training or injury.

Demands of the Sport

The demands of the sport must be considered when designing the plyometric program. Determine if the sport movements are mostly linear, vertical, lateral, or a combination of these movements. For example, volleyball players require vertical and lateral movement, while long jumpers emphasize horizontal movement. The intensity and volume should also be considered in the program design. For example, during a training phase an explosive athlete such as a shot-putter or discus thrower may use low volume and high intensity.

Equipment and Facilities

The equipment and facilities used plays a major role in power plyometrics training. Safety factors include: proper footwear, resilient surface, proper equipment and training area size. Footwear should provide sufficient ankle and arch support to prevent injury with cross-training shoes seen as the best for plyometrics. To prevent injuries, the landing surface should possess good shock-absorbing properties. The best surface is a flat (and dry) grass field. A good alternative would be wrestling mats. Wood, tile, concrete and carpet should be avoided due to their poor shock-absorbing properties. The size of the training area depends on the type of exercises being used. Long response drills may require a straightaway of 100 meters, where as bounding drills at least 30 meters. The boxes used for jumps should be sturdy, have a non-slip surface, and have rounded edges. For box jumps, adequate ceiling height must be provided.

Determining Volume and Intensity

Frequency, volume, intensity, progression and recovery all refer to the training session itself:

- **Frequency** is the number of workouts per week.
- **Volume** is the number of foot contacts per workout.
- **Intensity** refers to the amount of stress placed on the muscle during the workout. In most instances, power exercises are performed explosively from 1 to 6 seconds – utilizing the phosphate system.
- **Progression** is the change from low-intensity to medium-intensity to high-intensity levels as the athlete progresses.
- **Recovery** is the rest that is allowed between the individual sets of the drills. Plyometric drills should not be performed when an athlete is fatigued. Rest between sets must ensure complete recovery. In addition, power workouts should only be performed one to two times per week due to the high intensity nature of such workouts.

As volume relates to the number of foot contacts per workout, the following table is based upon an athlete who has sufficient base strength to begin plyometrics. The total number of sets, repetitions and rest intervals is dependent upon the intensity level of the drill, the sport, the time of the year and the fitness level of the athlete. Selection of the drills must be based on the required directional movements of the athlete.

Weeks	Drills	Sets x Reps	Rest Interval	Sessions
1 – 2	4 low intensity	2 x 10	2-3 minutes	2 x week
3 – 4	2 low, 2 medium	2 x 10	2-3 minutes	2 x week
5 – 6	4 medium	2-3 x 10	2-3 minutes	2 x week
7 – 8	2 medium, 2 high	med. 2–3 x 10 high 2 x 10	3 minutes	2 x week

THE BODY COACH

The volume of exercises for plyometrics is noted as sets and reps, the same as in weight training. The number of sets and reps refers to foot contacts. If a particular phase calls for 2 x 10, this refers to 2 sets of 10 foot contacts. The volume is determined by conditioning level and base strength. Low volume is considered to be 60–80 foot contacts, moderate 80–150 foot contacts, and high volume is 150–300 foot contacts. Upper body plyometrics follows similar principles.

Determining Intensity

Intensity (low, medium, or high) refers to the specific exercises being performed. **Low intensity** plyometric drills would be jump drills. Examples of these are jumps in place and standing jumps. **Moderate intensity** would include drills such as short-response hops, long-response hops, or combination jumps. Combination jumps are low-intensity jumps combined in a continuous pattern. **High-intensity** plyometrics are very advanced and should not be considered until after 6 weeks of low and moderate intensity drills have been accomplished. Examples of high-intensity drills are shocks, power jumps, and single leg hops. Shock jumps include in-depth jumps, box jumps, and medicine ball power drills.

Power Progression

No matter what one's age or ability level, power exercises need to start at a low to moderate level and be mastered before progressing along what is often referred to as a stress continuum. Mastering refers to the ability to perform each movement pattern with correct technique for the specific amount of repetitions or sets without losing form. The body itself is placed under extreme load from the forces of each exercise, which often go unnoticed; don't be fooled as the body its muscles, joints, tendons and nervous system all need time to develop and adjust. Each athlete therefore needs to spend time on each drill even though it may seem easy to perform at the time in order to allow the body (muscle, tendons, joints) and nervous system to adjust appropriately and motor coordination and technique to be mastered. In some instances, individual exercises may require 4-6 weeks of regular practice to master before progressing.

There is a method to power training that needs to be applied by all athletes for power improvements to occur. This comes from learning the finer details of each exercise, maintaining the correct body position throughout and the appropriate recovery periods. Once the body has adjusted, a new stress continuum (or level) of exercise can be introduced. The aim is introduce one level at a time and build from there. Successful power progression therefore relies on a step-by-step approach that requires patience from the athlete whilst they learn and apply the finer details of each exercise including the specific number of repetitions and sets and recovery periods required between each exercise and an understanding of the timeframe for the body to adjust accordingly to the stressors. The experience of a strength and conditioning coach is essential for any athlete or sporting team. Low intensity plyometric exercises can be incorporated into general circuit and weight training during the early stages of training so as to progressively condition the athlete. Simple plyometric drills such as skipping hopping and bounding may be introduced first. More demanding exercises such as flying start single-leg hops and depth jumps should be limited to thoroughly conditioned athletes in a highly supervised training environment.

Stress Continuum

If you stand with both feet together, then slightly bend your knees and jump into the air just a few inches and then land again, you have just performed a power exercise. Now, if you were to stand on one leg and perform the same movement you would see the power demand and stress levels have increased. This is one example of the stress continuum in practice. What each athlete must learn to understand is that power training in this instance is not about how much force (speed and strength) your body can generate – in the beginning its all about understanding what position your body

THE BODY COACH

should be in and how the force is applied and then absorbed (ie. jumping and then landing) ensuring correct technique. Once this is mastered total power is introduced as you can withstand the forces. I'll restress this point because in almost all power training exercises using one's bodyweight, a force is generated to start the exercise (ie. jumping) followed by an absorption phase (ie. landing), which can be repeated over and over again. In developing a good understanding of your body position in space and time you become more aware of the whole movement pattern from start to finish and the requirements of the body it's muscles and joints. Once good body awareness is achieved, this creates a better understanding of the forces being applied and absorbed. The example of hopping on two feet and then hopping using just one foot, performing the same exercise, provides a basic example of how an exercise is progressed along the stress continuum from easier to harder exercises with a higher demand on the body. This requires good posture, balance, stability, flexibility, core-strength and motor coordination. Another exercise example relates to how much force is applied when jumping followed by landing including height, length and power generated. As the stress continuum increases so to do the demands placed on the body, hence the body (muscles, joints, tendons etc) must have adapted appropriately to a lessor demand before moving on to a higher one.

Whilst many athletes may be able to perform an exercise once, the problem lies within the body and energy system which will not be able to handle the load or stress as a result of performing the exercise. The objective is to therefore focus on good posture, balance, stability, flexibility, core-strength motor coordination and quality of movement in all exercises as opposed to quantity to allow the body to adapt appropriately in the development of power by understanding the stress continuum model from low to high intensity.

Warm-up and Cooldown for Power Plyometric Exercises

Because of the explosive nature of power plyometrics, warm-up and cooldown periods are critical to a successful workout. Without proper warm-up, the possibility of joint or muscle injury may increase, therefore, decreasing performance. This warm-up should again emphasize posture, balance, flexibility, and stability. A warm-up routine should incorporate a general warm-up, dynamic flexibility and a specific warm-up, which mimics the athlete's common athletic movements, to ensure warmth of the core muscles and prepare and activate the musculoskeletal system. Not only will a proper warm-up raise core temperature, it will also increase excitation level of the nervous system, increase range of motion about joints, improve elasticity and contractile ability of muscles, shorten reaction time, and enhance overall coordination. Standard static stretches for the adductors, gluteus, hamstrings, thigh and calves can follow. Core warmth must be maintained, however, so static stretching should be kept to shorter periods and is best performed after a workout for an extended period to reduce muscle soreness and maintain flexibility levels. Cooling down should be the final portion of a plyometric session. A proper cooldown should include stretching, hydrotherapy, and nutrition to begin recovery and restoration of the musculoskeletal system. Proper warm-up and cooldown sessions will provide for successful plyometric sessions and aid in the recovery of the athlete afterwards.

Power Training Summary

In order for athletic improvements to be made, certain power progressions must exist. Athletes must be closely monitored by coaches, checking posture, balance, stability, flexibility, skill and motor coordination, before mastering an exercise and progressing to more intense ones. Only athletes who have already achieved high levels of strength through standard resistance training should engage in power plyometric drills.

The exercise should be specific to the athlete's sport. For example, sprinters would want to focus more on bounds while basketball and volleyball players perform more hops and jumps. Likewise, a plyometric program for a rugby forward may also want to stress the importance of upper body plyometric exercises. Adjustments must be made whenever needed.

Athletes must also understand that ground contact time must be kept as short as possible. Exercises should even be discontinued if the athlete is spending too much time on the ground or fatigued. Time for complete recovery should be allowed between plyometric exercise sets. A thorough set of warm-up exercises should be performed before beginning a power training session. Less demanding drills should be mastered prior to attempting more complex and intense drills. Ensure correct footwear is worn and landing surfaces have good shock absorbing qualities. Following these general power training principles will allow the athlete the greatest chance of success and athletic improvement.

Chapter 2

Power
Testing

Athletic competition is the ultimate test of performance capability, and is the best indication of training success. However, when trying to maximize athletic performance, it is important to determine the athlete's ability in individual aspects of performance. In this instance, we aim to measure individual components of performance in terms of power. These findings can be used as benchmarks to improve upon and can be used as a guide in designing an athletic training program.

The major benefit of testing is to establish the strengths and weaknesses of the athlete. This is done by comparing test results to other athletes in the same age group or sport. By comparing results you can see the areas which need improvement, and the training program can be modified accordingly. This way, valuable training time can be used more efficiently.

The initial testing session can give the athlete an idea of where their fitness levels are at the start of a program, so that future testing can be compared to this and any changes can be noted. A benchmark is especially important if you are about to embark on a new training phase. Subsequent tests should be planned for the end and start of each new training phase throughout the year. It usually takes a minimum of 4–6 weeks to see a demonstrable change in any aspect of fitness.

Ultimately, each power exercise within this book is a test within itself. The following 4 power tests provide a general overview to build upon. Remember, always warm up and stretch prior to performing any exercises or testing.

Test 1: **Standing Long Jump**

Aim
To monitor the development of an athlete's leg power in horizontal distance from a standing point.

Equipment required
- Flat grass area or long jump a pit
- Markers, tape measure and assistant
- Appropriate sporting footwear for proper grip and stability

Instruction
The athlete places their feet in line with markers or over the edge of the sandpit. The athlete squats, swings their arms backwards, then jumps forwards as far as possible – jumping off and landing on both feet. The coach should measure from the edge of the sandpit to the nearest point of contact. The start of the jump must be from a static position.

| Start | Jump | Land |

Performance Assessment
Assess the following areas:
1. Distance recorded in meters or centimeters.
2. Record scores of athletes in a team for comparison.
3. Assess motor coordination for improvement.

THE BODY COACH

Test 2: 3 Step Long Jump

Aim

To monitor the development of an athlete's leg power in horizontal distance from a 3 step run up.

Equipment required

- Long jump pit or flat grass area
- Markers, tape measure and Assistant
- Appropriate sporting footwear for proper grip and stability

Instruction

Stand 3 steps behind the line or edge of the sandpit. Run forwards 3 steps and jump off the favored leg as far as possible – landing on both feet. The coach should measure from the edge of the sandpit to the nearest point of contact.

3 Steps to Take-off Point   **Jump and Land**

Performance Assessment

Assess the following areas:

1. Distance recorded in meters or centimeters.
2. Record scores of athletes in a team for comparison.
3. Assess motor coordination for improvement.

Test 3: Standing Vertical Height Jump

Aim
To assess the power of the legs in projecting the body upwards. The subject jumps upwards as high as possible.

Equipment required
- Wall area
- Tape measure and assistant
- Appropriate sporting footwear for proper grip and stability

Instruction
Starting position: Stand beside a wall and mark the height of your extended arm.
Movement: Bend knees, swing arms back, then jump up as high as possible to mark the wall with the hand before landing with both feet together.

Mark End-range of Arm   **Lower**   **Jump and Touch**

Performance Assessment
Measure the distance between the two marks in centimeters (extended arm when standing and the height of the mark when jumping).

Jump (1): _____   Jump (2): _____

THE BODY COACH

Test 4: Flying Start Single Leg Hop

Aim
To monitor the development of an athlete's leg power in each leg, hip stability and muscle coordination.

Equipment required
- 25 meter area (or line)
- Dry, flat grass area or sprung wooden floor
- Markers, stop watch and assistant
- Appropriate sporting footwear for proper grip and stability

Instruction
The athlete starts 5 meters behind the starting line. Using a jogging run-up, the athlete starts hopping on the left leg from the first marker. The time taken to hop 20 meters between the two markers is recorded. Rest 3 minutes and then repeat the test by hopping on the right leg.

5 m jog   **20 m hop**

Flying Start   **Single Leg Hop**   **Hop 20 Meters**

Test 4: **Performance Assessment**

Assess the following areas:

1. Time recorded in seconds for:

   (a) Left leg = _____

   (b) Right leg = _____

2. Time difference between left and right leg hop

   = _____

   Which leg is more dominant – left or right?

3. Total number of hops over the 20 meter distance

   (a) Left leg = _____

   (b) Right leg = _____

4. Hip stability and motor coordination
   - Does the athlete maintain strong pelvic position whilst hopping?
   - Does the athlete have good or poor leg coordination?
   - What area(s) does the athlete need improve?

5. Record scores of athletes in a team for comparison

Note: This test can be performed over shorter or longer distances. Training is then adapted to suit the progressive nature of skill, motor coordination, fitness and flexibility. It is recommended that the correct hopping technique be learnt in a stationary position using both legs before distance or a number of continuous hops are introduced. The goal of this drill is maintaining excellent body posture, technique and motor coordination, without fatigue, over any set distance, starting from 5 meters up to a maximum of 50 meters.

Chapter 3

Jumps

Jumps are exercises that generally involve both legs during the take-off and the landing. A vertical jump in place aims for gaining maximum vertical height, whereas a horizontal jumps focuses on distance from starting point. As an athlete's strength, skill, posture and technique improves, single leg jumps are introduced due to the relationship in sporting activities such as long jump, high jump, triple jump and dunking a basketball.

1. POGO JUMP

Start **Midpoint**

INSTRUCTION

1. Stand tall with arms bent by side of body
2. Emphasize a vertical movement
3. Keep body tight from head-to-toe and flex and extend the ankle for control and stability
4. Maintain this motion to ensure sturdy contacts and quick, elastic takeoffs after landing
5. Use only the lower portion of the legs for jumping
6. Emphasize slight flexion and extension of the knee, and more flexion of the ankle and foot
7. Maintain good body posture at all times when jumping and landing as quality of movement is paramount over quantity

2. SQUAT JUMP

| Start | Midpoint |

INSTRUCTION

1. Start with feet shoulder-width apart in a half-squat position
2. Keep arms bent by side
3. Lower body by bending the knees and then explode upward as high as possible, extending the hips, knees, and ankles to maximize length as quickly as you can
4. Use arms to assist with upward drive and balance upon landing
5. Control the body position by bending the knees to absorb the landing
6. Ensure quality of movement at all times
7. Once landed, reset and begin another repetition, as required
8. Progress from the single response to the multiple response as strength and power improves
9. Work for maximum height for each jump
10. Maintain good body posture at all times when jumping and landing as quality of movement is paramount over quantity

3. BOX JUMP – SINGLE RESPONSE

Start   Midpoint

INSTRUCTION

1. Start with feet shoulder-width apart in a half-squat position in front of box
2. Keep arms bent by side
3. Lower body by bending the knees and then explode upward as high as possible, extending the hips, knees, and ankles to maximize length as quickly as you can
4. Land up on top of box platform with box feet
5. Bend knees to absorb the landing
6. Use arms to assist with upward drive and balance upon landing
7. Step down off box and repeat
8. Maintain good body posture at all times when jumping and landing as quality of movement is paramount over quantity

THE BODY COACH

4. MISSILE JUMP

| Start | Midpoint |

INSTRUCTION

1. Start with feet shoulder-width apart in a half-squat position
2. Keep arms bent by side
3. Lower body by bending the knees and then explode upward as high as possible
4. Extend the arms overhead and hips, knees and ankles to maximize length as quickly as you can
5. As the body lowers, absorb the shock by flexing the ankle and knee joints whilst lowering the arms
6. Maintain good body posture at all times when jumping and landing as quality of movement is paramount over quantity

5. STAR JUMP

Start   Midpoint

INSTRUCTION

1. Start with feet shoulder-width apart, legs slightly bent and arms bent by side
2. Lower body by bending the knees and then explode upward as high as possible
3. Extend the legs and arms outwards away from body
4. As the body lowers, bring arms and legs back to starting position
5. Absorb the shock by flexing the ankle and knee joints whilst lowering the arms
6. Maintain good body posture at all times when jumping and landing as quality of movement is paramount over quantity

THE BODY COACH

6. BUTT KICK

Start   Midpoint

INSTRUCTION

1. Start with feet shoulder-width apart, legs slightly bent and arms bent by side
2. Lower body by bending the knees and then explode upward
3. Simultaneously bring both heels towards buttocks and touch with hands
4. As the body lowers, bring arms and legs back to starting position
5. Absorb the shock by flexing the ankle and knee joints whilst lowering the arms
6. Maintain good body posture at all times when jumping and landing as quality of movement is paramount over quantity

7. DOUBLE LEG TUCK-JUMP

Start | **Midpoint**

INSTRUCTION

1. Start with feet shoulder-width apart, legs slightly bent and arms bent by side
2. Lower body by bending the knees and then explode upward
3. Simultaneously bring both knees up towards chest and touch knees with hands
4. As the body lowers, bring arms and legs back to starting position
5. Absorb the shock by flexing the ankle and knee joints whilst lowering the arms
6. Maintain good body posture at all times when jumping and landing as quality of movement is paramount over quantity

THE BODY COACH

8. SPLIT JUMP

Start	Midpoint

INSTRUCTION

1. Start in forward lunge position, arms by side
2. Simultaneously bend both knees and lower body then explode upwards straightening both legs in the air
3. Jump as high as possible vertically
4. As the body lowers, bring arms and legs back to starting position
5. Absorb the shock by flexing the ankle and knee joints whilst lowering the arms
6. Maintain good body posture at all times when jumping and landing as quality of movement is paramount over quantity
7. Switch legs and perform exercise with the opposite leg forward

9. SCISSORS JUMP

| Start | Midpoint |

INSTRUCTION
1. Start in forward lunge position, arms by side
2. Simultaneously bend both knees and lower body then explode upwards straightening both legs in the air
3. Jump as high as possible vertically
4. At the top of the jump in midair, rapidly reverse the position of the legs, changing the legs front to back and back to front
5. As the body lowers, bring arms and legs back to starting position
6. Absorb the shock by flexing the ankle and knee joints whilst lowering the arms
7. Maintain good body posture at all times when jumping and landing as quality of movement is paramount over quantity

NOTE
- ADVANCED: In a multiple response sequence, repeat the jump again reversing the position of the legs

10. ADVANCED DOUBLE SCISSORS JUMP

| Start | Midpoint |

INSTRUCTION

1. Start in forward lunge position, arms by side
2. Simultaneously bend both knees and lower body then explode upwards straightening both legs in the air
3. Jump as high as possible vertically
4. At the top of the jump in midair, perform double scissor switch rapidly, changing the legs front to back and back to front and then back again
5. As the body lowers, bring arms and legs back to starting position
6. Absorb the shock by flexing the ankle and knee joints whilst lowering the arms
7. Maintain good body posture at all times when jumping and landing as quality of movement is paramount over quantity

NOTE

• Recover after movement, then repeat with opposite leg forwards

11. TUCK-JUMP WITH HEEL KICK

| Start | Jump | Land |

INSTRUCTION
1. Stand with feet shoulder-width apart, knees slightly bent, with arms at sides
2. Jump up bringing heels to buttocks, keeping arms forwards to maintain balance
3. Land on balls of feet and repeat, if necessary
4. Remember to reduce ground contact time by landing softy on feet and springing into the air
5. Maintain good body posture at all times when jumping and landing as quality of movement is paramount over quantity

THE BODY COACH

12. SPLIT SQUAT JUMP

| Start | Jump | Land |

INSTRUCTION

1. Stand with feet shoulder-width apart; take right leg and step back approximately 2 feet standing on the ball of back foot
2. Feet should be positioned at a staggered stance with head and back erect and straight in a neutral position
3. Lower body by bending at hip and knee until thigh is parallel to floor then immediately explode vertically extending arms overhead
4. Prior to takeoff, extend the ankles to their maximum range (full plantar flexion) to ensure proper mechanics
5. Land on balls of feet and repeat, if necessary
6. Maintain good body posture at all times when jumping and landing as quality of movement is paramount over quantity

13. SPLIT SQUAT WITH CYCLE

| Start | Cycle | Land |

INSTRUCTION

1. Stand with feet shoulder-width apart; take right leg and step back approximately 2 feet standing on the ball of back foot
2. Feet should be positioned at a staggered stance with head and back erect and straight in a neutral position
3. Lower body by bending at hip and knee until thigh is parallel to floor then immediately explode vertically
4. Switch feet in the air so that the back foot lands forward and vice versa
5. Prior to take-off, extend the ankles to their maximum range (full plantar flexion) to ensure proper mechanics
6. Repeat with opposite leg forward in lunge position
7. Maintain good body posture at all times when jumping and landing as quality of movement is paramount over quantity

THE BODY COACH

14. SPLIT PIKE JUMP

| Start | Pike Jump | Land |

INSTRUCTION

1. Stand with feet shoulder-width apart, knees slightly bent, with arms at sides
2. Use a counter movement then jump up keeping legs straight and spread apart towards a parallel position with the ground – touching toes with hands
3. Land on balls of feet and repeat, if necessary
4. Remember to reduce ground contact time by landing softy on feet and springing into the air
5. Maintain good body posture at all times when jumping and landing as quality of movement is paramount over quantity

15. STRAIGHT PIKE JUMP

| Start | Pike Jump | Land |

INSTRUCTION

1. Stand with feet shoulder-width apart, knees slightly bent, with arms at sides
2. Jump up keeping legs straight and together towards a parallel position with ground – touching toes with hands
3. Land on balls of feet and repeat, if necessary
4. Remember to reduce ground contact time by landing softy on feet and springing into the air
5. Maintain good body posture at all times when jumping and landing as quality of movement is paramount over quantity

THE BODY COACH

16. STANDING LONG JUMP

| Start | Jump | Land |

INSTRUCTION
1. Stand with feet shoulder-width apart, in line with markers, knees slightly bent and arms at sides
2. Simultaneously squat, swing arms backwards, then jump forwards as far as possible
3. Jump and land with both feet together
4. Bend knees upon landing to absorb shock
5. Maintain good body posture at all times when jumping and landing as quality of movement is paramount

17. STANDING LONG JUMP WITH SPRINT

| Start | Jump and Land | Land |

INSTRUCTION

1. Stand with feet shoulder-width apart, in line with markers, knees slightly bent and arms at sides
2. Simultaneously squat, swing arms backwards, then jump forwards as far as possible
3. Jump and land with both feet together
4. Bend knees upon landing to absorb shock
5. React and sprint forwards 10 meters
6. Maintain good body posture at all times when jumping and landing as quality of movement is paramount

THE BODY COACH

18. STANDING LONG JUMP WITH LATERAL SPRINT

| Start | Jump and Land | Sprint Laterally |

INSTRUCTION
1. Stand with feet shoulder-width apart, in line with markers, knees slightly bent and arms at sides
2. Simultaneously squat, swing arms backwards, then jump forwards as far as possible
3. Jump and land with both feet together
4. Bend knees upon landing to absorb shock
5. React and sprint laterally 10 meters
6. Vary directions with each jump
7. Maintain good body posture at all times when jumping and landing as quality of movement is paramount

19. STANDING JUMP OVER MARKER

| Start | Jump | Land |

INSTRUCTION

1. Stand 1-2 feet away from marker
2. Feet should be slightly wider than hip-width apart in a semi-squat position and arms at sides
3. Simultaneously squat, swing arms backwards, then jump up and over marker
4. Jumping and land with both feet together
5. Bend knees upon landing to absorb shock
6. This is a single jump only
7. Maintain good body posture at all times when jumping and landing as quality of movement is paramount over quantity

20. 1-2-3 DRILL

| Step 1 | Step 2 | Step 3 |

INSTRUCTION

1. Step 1: Run forward in a running motion
2. Step 2: Repeat running motion on opposite side
3. Step 3: On third action jump high into the air
4. Land a repeat steps 1 to 3 again, over set distance
5. Movement is 1, 2, 3 jump
6. Maintain good body posture at all times when jumping and landing as quality of movement is paramount over quantity

21. 180-DEGREE JUMPS

| Start | Jump | Land |

INSTRUCTION
1. Stand 1-2 feet away from marker
2. Feet should be slightly wider than hip-width apart in a semi-squat position and arms at sides
3. Simultaneously squat, swing arms backwards, then jump up – rotating body 180-degrees in the air – up and over marker
4. Land on opposite side of marker facing the opposite direction
5. Bend knees upon landing to absorb shock
6. Jump and land with both feet together
7. This is a single jump only
8. Rest and repeat in opposite direction
9. Maintain good body posture at all times when jumping and landing as quality of movement is paramount over quantity

22. LATERAL JUMP – SINGLE LEG

| Start | Jump | Land |

INSTRUCTION

1. Stand on single leg with arms by side
2. Simultaneously squat, swing arms backwards, then jump up laterally to the side
3. Land on same leg
4. Bend knees upon landing to absorb shock
5. This can be a single jump or double jump – back and forth
6. Multiple continuous jumps are for advanced athletes only
7. Repeat action standing on opposite leg
8. Maintain good body posture at all times when jumping and landing as quality of movement is paramount over quantity

23. LATERAL JUMP OVER MARKER

| Start | Jump | Land |

INSTRUCTION

1. Stand on single leg 1-2 feet away from marker with arms by side
2. Simultaneously squat, swing arms backwards, then jump up laterally – to the side – up and over marker
3. Land on same leg
4. Bend knees upon landing to absorb shock
5. This can be a single jump or double jump – back and forth
6. Multiple continuous jumps are for advanced athletes only
7. Repeat action standing on opposite leg
8. Maintain good body posture at all times when jumping and landing as quality of movement is paramount over quantity

THE BODY COACH

24. 3-STEP LONG JUMP

| 3 Steps to Take-off | Jump and Land |

INSTRUCTION
1. Stand 3 steps behind line or edge of the sandpit.
2. Run forwards 3 steps and jump off favored leg as far as possible
3. Extend legs forward and land with both feet together
4. Rest up to 5 minutes before repeating this exercise as it requires explosive bursts
5. Maintain good body posture at all times when jumping and landing as quality of movement is paramount over quantity

25. STANDING TRIPLE JUMP

| Start | Jump | Land |

INSTRUCTION

1. Start by standing on favored leg next to markers
2. Bend opposite leg off the ground and arms by side
3. Hop forwards on same leg
4. Then step forwards on opposite leg with big lunge
5. Land on opposite leg and jump
6. Bring both feet together in the air and lean forwards maintaining balance with arms
7. Land on both feet
8. Rest up to 5 minutes before repeating this exercise as it requires explosive bursts
9. Maintain good body posture at all times when jumping and landing as quality of movement is paramount over quantity

THE BODY COACH

Chapter 4

Bounds

Bounds involve movements from one leg to the other with the primary emphasis on gaining maximum horizontal distance and vertical height being a factor in the success of that distance. Bounds are normally measured in distance such as short-response up to 30 meters and long response beyond this distance.

26. BOUND

Start | **Bounce Forwards**

INSTRUCTION

1. Jog into the start of the drill for forward momentum
2. After a few feet, forcefully push off with the left foot and bring the leg forward at same time driving your right arm forward
3. Repeat with other leg and arm
4. This exercise is an exaggerated running motion focusing on foot push-off and air time
5. The upper body action is the same as in running
6. Complete over a set amount of bounds or distance
7. Maintain good body posture at all times when jumping and landing as quality of movement is paramount over quantity

27. GALLOP

| Start | Reaction |

INSTRUCTION

1. Begin by pushing with off with the back leg and the foot, keeping the ankle locked to emphasize a spring-loaded landing and take-off
2. Continue to keep the same leg behind the hips and project the hips forward, while maintaining the opposite leg in a forward position for initial landing and balance within each stride
3. Emphasize hip projections upward and forward with forceful, quick extensions of the back knee and ankle, accompanied by light, cyclic striding actions of the lead leg
4. After executing 6-10 repetitions, switch the position of the legs and repeat the sequence
5. Maintain good body posture at all times when jumping and landing as quality of movement is paramount over quantity

28. LATERAL BOUND – SINGLE RESPONSE

Push Off | Bound Across

INSTRUCTION

1. Start by standing on right leg with arms by side
2. Bound across laterally to left leg, emphasizing distance and horizontal trajectory
3. Trail landing on left leg with right foot to touch ground next to left foot
4. Immediately react and bound off left leg back across to the right side
5. Trail landing on right leg with left foot to touch ground next to right foot
6. The lead foot will land first with the trail foot following to balance the landing
7. Absorb bound by slightly bending the knee
8. Repeat movement from one side across to the other and back, then rest
9. Maintain good body posture at all times when jumping and landing as quality of movement is paramount over quantity

THE BODY COACH

29. LATERAL BOUND – MULTIPLE RESPONSE

| Bound | Mid-air | Land |

INSTRUCTION

1. Start by standing on right leg with arms by side
2. Bound across laterally to left leg, emphasizing distance and horizontal trajectory
3. Trail landing on left leg with right foot to touch ground next to left foot
4. Upon landing, drive off again in the opposite direction, quickly and powerfully, returning to the distance you began
5. Immediately react and bound off left leg back across to the right side
6. Trail landing on right leg with left foot to touch ground next to right foot
7. The lead foot will land first with the trail foot following to balance the landing
8. Absorb bound by slightly bending the knee
9. Repeat movement back and forth for a set amount of repetitions
10. Maintain good body posture at all times when jumping and landing as quality of movement is paramount over quantity

30. ALTERNATE-LEG BOUND

Balance on One Leg   **On Go, React and Sprint**

INSTRUCTION

1. Begin by pushing off with the back leg, driving the knee forward and upward to gain as much height and distance as possible before landing
2. Repeat the sequence, driving up with the other leg
3. Think about hanging in the air to increase distance, with knee high
4. Keep the ankle locked in dorsiflexion and the heel up under the hips to reduce the ground-contact time and promote efficient hip projection upon subsequent take-off
5. Alternate arm action is preferred but a double arm action may be used
6. Repeat movement over set amount of bounds or distance
7. Maintain good body posture at all times when jumping and landing as quality of movement is paramount over quantity

THE BODY COACH

31. ALTERNATE-LEG DIAGONAL BOUND

| Bound to Left | Bound to Right |

INSTRUCTION

1. Utilize straight line, if available
2. Begin by pushing off with the back leg, driving the knee forward and upward increasing the distance from side to side as well as forward
3. Landing on opposite side of line, repeat the sequence, driving up with the other leg
4. Think about hanging in the air to increase distance, with knee high
5. Keep the ankle locked in dorsiflexion and the heel up under the hips to reduce the ground-contact time and promote efficient hip projection upon subsequent take-off – in a forward diagonal pattern
6. Alternate arm action is preferred but a double arm action may be used
7. Repeat movement over set amount of bounds or distance
8. Maintain good body posture at all times when jumping and landing as quality of movement is paramount over quantity

32. BOX BOUND

| Start | Step | Bound | Land |

INSTRUCTION (for advanced athletes only)

1. Stand behind box
2. Bounds forwards with left foot landing on box platform
3. Bound immediately off left foot forwards and up into air with legs cycling
4. Maintain an erect torso and allow immediate forward hip projection
5. Land in forward lunge position on opposite leg – absorbing the forces by bending the knees and using arms for balance
6. Rest for up to 5 minutes for full recovery
7. Repeat sequence, bounding off right leg from box
8. Maintain good body posture at all times when jumping and landing as quality of movement is paramount over quantity

THE BODY COACH

Chapter 5

Hops

Hops are take-off and landing movements from one leg onto the same leg or two-feet take-off with two-foot landings. Hops are repeated over a specific distance or certain number of repetitions. These include short-response hops up to 10 repetitions and long-response hop for 20-30 meters or more. Balance and postural control are important in the early progressions of hops for developing good motor coordination.

33. TWO-FOOT ANKLE HOP

| Start | Ankle Hop |

INSTRUCTION
1. Stand tall with arms bent by side of body
2. Slightly bend legs and hip region
3. Hop up with primary motion at ankle joint
4. Emphasize a vertical movement
5. Keep body tight from head-to-toe and flex and extend the ankle for control and stability
6. Maintain this motion to ensure sturdy contacts and quick, elastic takeoffs after landing
7. Use only the lower portion of the legs for jumping
8. Emphasize slight flexion and extension of the knee, and more flexion of the ankle and foot
9. Maintain good body posture at all times when jumping and landing as quality of movement is paramount over quantity

THE BODY COACH

34. SINGLE FOOT SIDE-TO-SIDE ANKLE HOP

Balance on One Leg   **Side-to-Side Hop**

INSTRUCTION

1. Note: Markers are used to show movement from side-to-side
2. Stand on left leg with arms by side
3. Start with counter movement – squat, swing arms backwards
4. Hop across laterally with the primary action at ankle joint
5. Land on same leg
6. Bend knees upon landing to absorb shock and repeat action hopping back across to starting point
7. Continue single foot hop from side-to-side for set number of repetitions
8. Rest and then repeat action standing on right leg
9. Maintain good body posture at all times when jumping and landing as quality of movement is paramount over quantity

35. SIDE-TO-SIDE ANKLE HOP

| Start | Ankle Hop | Land |

INSTRUCTION

1. Stand with feet together and arms bent by side
2. Start with counter movement – squat, swing arms backwards
3. Hop across laterally on both feet with the primary action at ankle joint
4. Bend knees upon landing to absorb shock and repeat action hopping back across to starting point
5. Continue foot hops from side-to-side for set number of repetitions
6. Maintain good body posture at all times when jumping and landing as quality of movement is paramount over quantity

36. HIP-TWIST ANKLE HOP

| Start | Midpoint | Land |

INSTRUCTION

1. Stand with feet together and arms bent by side
2. Start with counter movement – squat, swing arms backwards
3. Hop up and twist body to a 45-degree angle to the left side from starting point with the primary action at ankle joint
4. Bend knees upon landing to absorb shock and repeat action hopping back across to the opposite side 45-degrees beyond starting point to the right side
5. Continue foot hops from side-to-side for set number of repetitions
6. Maintain good body posture at all times when jumping and landing as quality of movement is paramount over quantity

37. DOUBLE-LEG MULTIPLE HOP

| Start | Land | Land and Reset |

INSTRUCTION

1. Set 3-6 boxes 1-2 meters apart, or as required by athlete
2. Stand behind box with feet close, legs slightly bent and arms by side
3. Start with counter movement – squat, swing arms backwards
4. Hop forwards on both feet, up and over box
5. Upon clearing the first box, land with full-foot contact and give at the knees and hips
6. Use arms for balance and control
7. After sticking this first landing, pause, then reset the body position, stance, and relationship to the next box.
8. Repeat forward action
9. Maintain good body posture at all times when jumping and landing as quality of movement is paramount over quantity

THE BODY COACH

38. DOUBLE-LEG SPEED HOP

| Hop | Land | Hop |

INSTRUCTION (for advanced athletes only)
1. Set 3-6 boxes 1-2 meters apart, or as required by athlete
2. Stand behind box with feet close, legs slightly bent and arms by side
3. Start with counter movement – squat, swing arms backwards
4. Hop forwards on both feet, up and over box
5. Upon clearing the first box, land with full-foot contact and give at the knees and hips – use arms for balance and control
6. Upon each landing, take off quickly upward again with the same cycling hop action of the legs
7. Execute the action sequence as rapidly as possible
8. Work for height and distance, but not at the expense of poor technique
9. Maintain good body posture at all times when jumping and landing as quality of movement is paramount over quantity

39. SIDE HOP

| Start | Hop | Land |

INSTRUCTION (for advanced athletes only)

1. Set boxes 1-2 meters apart, or as required by athlete
2. Stand behind box in lateral position with feet close, legs slightly bent and arms by side
3. Start with counter movement – squat, swing arms backwards
4. Hop sideways over first box with both feet together, then the second box
5. Upon each landing, take off quickly upward again with the same cycling hop action of the legs – use arms for balance and control
6. Without hesitating, change direction by jumping back over the second box, then the first one
7. Continue this back-and-forth sequence for set amount of repetitions.
8. Maintain good body posture at all times when jumping and landing as quality of movement is paramount over quantity

THE BODY COACH

40. SIDE HOP WITH SPRINT

| Hop | Land | Sprint |

INSTRUCTION (for advanced athletes only)
1. Set boxes 1-2 meters apart, or as required by athlete
2. Stand behind box in lateral position with feet close, legs slightly bent and arms by side
3. Start with counter movement – squat, swing arms backwards
4. Hop sideways over first box with both feet together
5. Upon each landing, take off quickly upward again with the same cycling hop action of the legs – use arms for balance and control
6. Without hesitating, change direction by jumping back over first box to starting point
7. Continue this back-and-forth sequence for set amount of repetitions
8. Anticipate the landing on the last repetition; land in a sprint start posture and accelerate forward past a designated finish line 10-20 m away
9. This is a primary objective of the drill, as the emphasis is not the height of the hops but rather the rate of execution
10. Maintain good body posture at all times when jumping and landing as quality of movement is paramount over quantity

41. ZIG-ZAG HOP

| Hop Diagonally | Land | Hop Diagonally |

INSTRUCTION (for advanced athletes only)
1. Stand behind series of boxes with feet close, legs slightly bent and arms by side
2. Start with counter movement – squat, swing arms backwards
3. Hop diagonally forwards on both feet, up and over box to right side
4. Upon clearing the first box, land with full-foot contact and give at the knees and hips – use arms for balance and control
5. Upon each landing, take off quickly upward again with the same cycling hop action of the legs diagonally forwards across to left side
6. Execute the action sequence emphasizing a rapid side-to-side motion
7. Avoid 'double hopping' upon each landing and keep ground contact time to a minimum
8. Once skill has improved, progress to more distant angles and over an extended distance
9. Maintain good body posture at all times when jumping and landing as quality of movement is paramount over quantity

THE BODY COACH

42. SINGLE-LEG BUTT KICK

| Start | Butt Kick |

INSTRUCTION

1. Stand with feet shoulder-width apart, knees slightly bent, with arms at sides
2. Start with a counter movement, then jump up extending the hips for vertical height
3. Tuck the toes and heel of one leg upward and slightly backward into the buttocks
4. The knee will have a minimal rise upward and forward but not in a tuck manner
5. Land on balls of feet and repeat, if necessary for a set amount of repetitions
6. Remember to reduce ground contact time by landing softly on feet and springing into the air
7. Maintain good body posture at all times when jumping and landing as quality of movement is paramount over quantity

| Start | Hop | Land |

INSTRUCTION (for advanced athletes only)

1. Set 3-6 boxes 1-2 meters apart, or as required by athlete
2. Stand behind box on left leg, leg slightly bent and arms by side
3. Start with counter movement – squat, swing arms backwards
4. Hop forwards on left leg, up and over box
5. Upon clearing the first box, land with full-foot contact and give at the knees and hips – use arms for balance and control
6. Upon each landing, take off quickly upward again with the same cycling hop action of the leg
7. Execute the action sequence as rapidly as possible
8. Work for height and distance, but not at the expense of poor technique
9. Rest 3 minutes and repeat with right leg
10. Maintain good body posture at all times when jumping and landing as quality of movement is paramount over quantity

44. SINGLE-LEG LATERAL HOP

| Start | Hop | Land |

INSTRUCTION (for advanced athletes only)
1. Set boxes 1-2 meters apart, or as required by athlete
2. Stand behind box in a lateral position on left leg, legs slightly bent and arms by side
3. Start with counter movement – squat, swing arms backwards
4. Hop sideways over first box, then the second box
5. Upon each landing, take off quickly upward again with the same cycling hop action of the legs – use arms for balance and control
6. Without hesitating, change direction by jumping back over the second box, then the first one
7. Rest 3 minutes and repeat using right leg
8. Maintain good body posture at all times when jumping and landing as quality of movement is paramount over quantity

45. SINGLE-LEG SPEED HOP

| Start | Hop | Continue |

INSTRUCTION

1. Stand on left leg next to marker, legs slightly bent and arms by side
2. Start with counter movement – squat, swing arms backwards
3. Hop forwards on left leg
4. Upon each landing, take off quickly upward again with the same cycling hop action of the legs – use arms for balance and control
5. Use the multiple-response action of rapid yet fully explosive cyclic action for height and distance
6. Perform single leg hop over 10–20 meters
7. Maintain good body posture and technique at all times when jumping and landing as quality of movement is paramount over quantity
8. Rest 3 minutes and repeat using right leg

THE BODY COACH

46. FORWARD MARKER HOPS

| Start | Hop | Land |

INSTRUCTION

1. Set markers 1-2 meters apart over 10-20 meters, or as required by athlete
2. Stand behind markers with feet close, legs slightly bent and arms by side
3. Start with counter movement – squat, swing arms backwards
4. Hop forwards on both feet, up and over markers
5. Upon each landing, take off quickly upward again with the same cycling hop action of the legs – use arms for balance and control
6. Execute the action sequence as rapidly as possible
7. Work on speed of movement, but not at the expense of poor technique
8. Maintain good body posture at all times when jumping and landing as quality of movement is paramount over quantity

47. FORWARD MARKER HOPS WITH CHANGE OF DIRECTION SPRINT

| Start | Hop | Sprint Laterally |

INSTRUCTION

1. Set markers 1-2 meters apart over 10-20 meters, or as required by athlete
2. Stand behind markers with feet close, legs slightly bent and arms by side
3. Start with counter movement – squat, swing arms backwards
4. Hop forwards on both feet, up and over markers
5. Upon each landing, take off quickly upward again with the same cycling hop action of the legs – use arms for balance and control
6. Anticipate the landing on set hop; land in a sprint start posture and accelerate forward past a designated finish line 10-20 m away
7. Work on speed of movement, but not at the expense of poor technique
8. Maintain good body posture at all times when jumping and landing as quality of movement is paramount over quantity

THE BODY COACH

48. DOUBLE-LEG ZIG-ZAG HOP

| Hop | Land | Hop |

INSTRUCTION (for advanced athletes only)
1. Place 5-10 markers 0.5 – 2 meters apart in a zig-zag pattern
2. Stand behind first marker with feet close, legs slightly bent and arms by side
3. Start with counter movement – squat, swing arms backwards
4. Hop diagonally forwards on both feet, to diagonal marker
5. Land with full-foot contact and give at the knees and hips – use arms for balance and control
6. Upon each landing, take off quickly upward again with the same cycling hop action of the legs diagonally forwards across to the next marker
7. Execute the action sequence emphasizing a rapid zig-zag motion
8. Avoid 'double hopping' upon each landing and keep ground contact time to a minimum
9. Once skill has improved, progress to more distant angles and over an extended distance
10. Maintain good body posture at all times when jumping and landing as quality of movement is paramount over quantity

49. MARKER HOPS WITH CHANGE OF DIRECTION

| Start | Jump | Sprint |

INSTRUCTION

1. Stand behind single marker – feet close, legs slightly bent and arms by side
2. Start with counter movement – squat, swing arms backwards
3. Hop forwards on both feet, up and over marker
4. Land and then jump backwards over marker
5. Continue this back-and-forth sequence for a set amount of repetitions
6. Anticipate the landing on set hop; land, establish sprint start posture and accelerate forward past a designated finish line 10-20 m away
7. Work on speed of movement, but not at the expense of poor technique
8. Vary direction of sprint with each set
9. Maintain good body posture at all times when jumping and landing as quality of movement is paramount over quantity

50. 180-DEGREE TURN MARKER HOP WITH SPRINT

| Start | 180-degree Turn | Sprint |

INSTRUCTION (for advanced athletes only)

1. Stand 1-2 feet away from marker.
2. Feet should be slightly wider than hip-width apart in a semi-squat position and arms at sides
3. Simultaneously squat, swing arms backwards, then jump up – rotating body 180-degrees in the air – up and over marker
4. Land on opposite side of marker facing the opposite direction
5. Bend knees upon landing to absorb shock
6. Jump and land with both feet together – single jump only
7. Anticipate the landing on set hop; land in a sprint start posture and accelerate forward past a designated finish line 10-20 m away
8. Maintain good body posture at all times when jumping and landing as quality of movement is paramount over quantity.

51. DOUBLE LEG HOPS

| Start | Hop | Land |

INSTRUCTION

1. Start with feet shoulder-width apart, legs slightly bent and arms bent by side
2. Lower body by bending the knees and then explode upward
3. Simultaneously bring both knees up towards chest
4. As the body lowers, bring arms and legs back to starting position
5. Absorb the shock by flexing the ankle and knee joints whilst lowering the arms
6. Upon each landing, take off quickly upward again with the same action
7. Repeat for a set amount of repetitions
8. Maintain good body posture at all times when jumping and landing as quality of movement is paramount over quantity

THE BODY COACH

52. LATERAL MARKER HOPS

| Start | Jump | Land |

INSTRUCTION

1. Set markers 1-2 meters apart over 10-20 meters
2. Stand behind markers with feet close in a lateral position, legs slightly bent and arms by side
3. Start with counter movement – squat, swing arms backwards
4. Then hop laterally – to the side – up and over marker
5. Bend knees upon landing to absorb shock
6. Upon each landing, take off quickly upward again with the same action
7. Maintain good body posture at all times when jumping and landing as quality of movement is paramount over quantity
8. Rest 3 minutes and repeat action in opposite direction

53. LATERAL MARKER HOPS WITH SPRINT

Start   **Hop**   **Sprint**

INSTRUCTION

1. Set markers 1-2 meters apart over 10 meters
2. Stand behind markers with feet close in a lateral position, legs slightly bent and arms by side
3. Start with counter movement – squat, swing arms backwards
4. Then hop laterally – to the side – up and over marker
5. Bend knees upon landing to absorb shock
6. Upon each landing, take off quickly upward again with the same action
7. Anticipate the landing on set hop; land in a sprint start posture and accelerate forward past a designated finish line 10-20 m away
8. Work on speed of movement, but not at the expense of poor technique
9. Maintain good body posture at all times when jumping and landing as quality of movement is paramount over quantity.
10. Rest 3 minutes and repeat action in opposite direction

54. SINGLE LEG LATERAL MARKER HOPS

Start	Jump	Land

INSTRUCTION (for advanced athletes only)
1. Set markers 1-2 meters apart over 10-20 meters
2. Stand behind markers on left leg in a lateral position, legs slightly bent and arms by side
3. Start with counter movement – squat, swing arms backwards
4. Then hop laterally – to the side – up and over marker
5. Bend knees upon landing to absorb shock
6. Upon each landing, take off quickly upward again with the same action
7. Maintain good body posture at all times when jumping and landing as quality of movement is paramount over quantity
8. Rest 3 minutes and repeat action in opposite direction on right leg

55. SINGLE LEG LATERAL MARKER HOPS WITH SPRINT

| Start | Hop | Land and Sprint |

INSTRUCTION (for advanced athletes only)
1. Set markers 1-2 meters apart over 10-20 meters
2. Stand behind markers on left leg in a lateral position, legs slightly bent and arms by side
3. Start with counter movement – squat, swing arms backwards
4. Then hop laterally – to the side – up and over marker
5. Bend knees upon landing to absorb shock
6. Upon each landing, take off quickly upward again with the same action
7. Anticipate the landing on set hop; land in a sprint start posture and accelerate forward past a designated finish line 10-20 m away
8. Work on speed of movement, but not at the expense of poor technique
9. Maintain good body posture at all times when jumping and landing as quality of movement is paramount over quantity
10. Rest 3 minutes and repeat action in opposite direction

56. SINGLE LEG HOPS

| Hop | Land | Hop |

INSTRUCTION (for advanced athletes only)
1. Stand on right leg, slightly bent, and arms by side
2. Start with counter movement
3. Simultaneously, bend leg then explode upwards
4. Jump as high as possible vertically raising one knee forwards and the opposite heel towards buttocks
5. As the body lowers, bring arms and legs back to starting position
6. Absorb the shock by flexing the ankle and knee joints whilst lowering the arms
7. Maintain good body posture at all times when jumping and landing as quality of movement is paramount over quantity
8. Advanced: Upon each landing, take off quickly upward again with the same cycling hop action of the leg for set amount of repetitions
9. Execute the action sequence as rapidly as possible
10. Work for height, but not at the expense of poor technique
11. Rest 3 minutes and repeat with left leg

57. SINGLE LEG MULTIPLE MARKER HOPS

Start	Hop	Land

INSTRUCTION (for advanced athletes only)

1. Set markers 1-2 meters apart, or as required by athlete over 10 meters
2. Stand behind marker on left leg, leg slightly bent and arms by side
3. Start with counter movement – squat, swing arms backwards
4. Hop forwards on left leg, up and over marker
5. Upon clearing the first marker, land with full-foot contact and give at the knees and hips – use arms for balance and control
6. Upon each landing, take off quickly upward again with the same cycling hop action of the leg
7. Execute the action sequence as rapidly as possible
8. Work on speed, but not at the expense of poor technique
9. Maintain good body posture at all times when jumping and landing as quality of movement is paramount over quantity
10. Rest 3 minutes and repeat with right leg

THE BODY COACH

58. HURDLE HOPPING

| Hop | Land |

INSTRUCTION

1. Set up 5-10 hurdles approximately 1–2 meters apart, or as required by athlete
2. Stand behind hurdles with feet close, legs slightly bent and arms by side
3. Start with counter movement – squat, swing arms backwards
4. Hop forwards up and over hurdles on both feet
5. Tuck both knees to your chest
6. Use a double arm swing to maintain balance and gain height
7. Land on the balls of the feet, allowing energy to be stored by the elastic components of the leg muscles, reset and repeat hop
8. Maintain good body posture at all times when jumping and landing as quality of movement is paramount over quantity
9. Advanced athletes: land and immediately take off again over next hurdle – use arms for balance and control
10. Keep the feet touch down time between hurdles to the shortest time possible

Chapter 6

Box Drills

Plyometrics utilize the forces of gravity to store potential energy in the muscles, and then quickly turn this stored energy into kinetic energy. When you jump off a box and land on the ground, the muscles in your legs contract eccentrically to slow your body down. Then, when you jump forward your muscles contract concentrically to spring you off the ground. As the athlete steps off the box and lands, legs coiled, potential energy is stored, and as he then quickly leaps to the next box, kinetic energy is utilized. Power training basics focuses on a box height of 30-50 centimeters and expert coaching and supervision is required. Various box drills are also available in other chapters.

59. SINGLE LEG PUSH-OFF

| Start | Midpoint | Land |

INSTRUCTION

1. Stand behind box, with left leg on the box and right leg on the ground, arms by side
2. Using double arm action jump up using the foot on the box to push off
3. Land with the jump foot on the box, just before back foot touches the ground
4. Reset legs and repeat movement
5. Maintain good body posture at all times when jumping and landing as quality of movement is paramount over quantity
6. Advanced: Upon each landing, take off quickly upward again with the same cycling hop action of the leg
7. Rest 3 minutes and repeat with right leg starting on the box

60. UPS AND DOWNS

| Start | Midpoint | Jump |

INSTRUCTION
1. Stand on box with legs slightly bent and arms by side
2. Start with counter movement – bend knees, swing arms backwards and drop off box with feet landing on either side
3. Upon each landing, take off quickly upward again with hop action to land on top of box
4. Reset legs and repeat movement
5. Maintain good body posture at all times when jumping and landing as quality of movement is paramount over quantity.
6. Advanced: Perform multiple contacts or number of repetitions

THE BODY COACH

61. LATERAL BOX JUMP

| Start | Jump on Box | Land and Repeat |

INSTRUCTION

1. Stand 1 meter from box in lateral position, legs slightly bent and arms by side
2. Start with counter movement – squat, swing arms backwards
3. Hop sideways up and onto box, landing with both feet together
4. Upon each landing, take off quickly sideways to the ground keeping both feet close together – use arms for balance and control
5. Without hesitating, change direction by jumping back up onto the box and back to starting position
6. Continue this back-and-forth sequence for set amount of repetitions
7. Maintain good body posture at all times when jumping and landing as quality of movement is paramount over quantity

62. BOX JUMP – MULTIPLE RESPONSE

| Start | Midpoint | Landing |

INSTRUCTION

1. Start with feet shoulder-width apart in a half-squat position in front of box with arms bent by side
2. Lower body by bending the knees and then explode upwards
3. Land with feet simultaneously on top of the box or platform; immediately drop or jump back down to the original starting position
4. Repeat sequence, as required
5. Focus on keeping ground-contact (foot) time to a minimum
6. For variation, change directions of jumping and dropping off or onto platform
7. Maintain good body posture at all times when jumping and landing as quality of movement is paramount over quantity

THE BODY COACH

63. BOX JUMP EXPLOSION

| Start | Midpoint | Jump, Extend and Land |

INSTRUCTION

1. Start with feet shoulder-width apart in a half-squat position in front of box with arms bent by side
2. Lower body by bending the knees and then explode upwards, extending the hips, knees, and ankles and land up on top of box with both feet
3. Bend knees to absorb the landing
4. Use arms to assist with upward drive and balance upon landing, preparing for next take-off movement
5. Reset body for second explosive movement – squat, jump and extend arms overhead
6. Upon landing absorb shock by bending the knees and lowering the arms for balance
7. Maintain good body posture at all times when jumping and landing as quality of movement is paramount over quantity

NOTE

- ADVANCED: You can perform a variation of this exercise by landing on the box with only one foot, thus executing the leap with one driving leg before landing on both feet again

Start | **Land on Box** | **Step Forward and Land**

INSTRUCTION

1. Start with feet shoulder-width apart in front of 5 boxes set 1-2 meters apart with arms bent by side
2. Lower body by bending the knees and then explode upwards
3. Land with feet simultaneously on top of the box or platform
4. Step off platform, land on both feet and explode by jumping up onto next box
5. Repeat sequence along length of boxes
6. Maintain good body posture at all times when jumping and landing as quality of movement is paramount over quantity

THE BODY COACH

65. MULTIPLE BOX-TO-BOX JUMPS WITH SPRINT

| Start | Jump | Land and Sprint |

INSTRUCTION
1. Start with feet shoulder-width apart in front of 5 boxes set 1-2 meters apart with arms bent by side
2. Lower body by bending the knees and then explode upwards
3. Land with feet simultaneously on top of the box or platform
4. Step off platform, land on both feet and explode by jumping up onto next box
5. Repeat sequence along length of boxes
6. Off the final box, land in a sprint start posture and accelerate forward past a designated finish line 10–20 meters away
7. Maintain good body posture at all times when jumping and landing as quality of movement is paramount over quantity

66. MULTIPLE BARRIER HOPS WITH SPRINT

| Hop and Land | Hop | Land and Sprint |

INSTRUCTION (for advanced athletes only)
1. Stand behind 2 boxes, 1-2 meters apart, or as required by athlete with feet close, legs slightly bent and arms by side
2. Start with counter movement – squat, swing arms backwards
3. Hop forwards on both feet, up and over box
4. Upon clearing the first box, land with full-foot contact and give at the knees and hips – use arms for balance and control
5. Upon each landing, take off quickly upward again with the same cycling hop action of the legs over second box
6. Anticipate the landing
7. Land in a sprint start posture and accelerate forward past a designated finish line 10-20 m away
8. Execute the action sequence as rapidly as possible
9. Maintain good body posture at all times when jumping and landing as quality of movement is paramount over quantity

THE BODY COACH

67. MULTIPLE SINGLE LEG BOX HOPS WITH SPRINT

| Hop | Land | Sprint |

INSTRUCTION (for advanced athletes only)

1. Set 2 boxes 1-2 meters apart, or as required by athlete
2. Stand behind box on left leg, leg slightly bent and arms by side
3. Start with counter movement – squat, swing arms backwards
4. Hop forwards on left leg, up and over box
5. Upon clearing the first box, land with full-foot contact and give at the knees and hips – use arms for balance and control
6. Upon each landing, take off quickly upward again with the same cycling hop action of the leg
7. Anticipate the landing
8. Land in a sprint start posture and accelerate forward past a designated finish line 10-20 m away
9. Execute the action sequence as rapidly as possible.
10. Maintain good body posture at all times when jumping and landing as quality of movement is paramount over quantity
11. Rest 3 minutes and repeat with right leg

PROGRESSION TO DEPTH JUMP
68. JUMP TO BOX

| Start | Jump | Land |

INSTRUCTION

1. Start with feet shoulder-width apart in front of box with arms bent by side
2. Lower body by bending the knees and then explode upwards driving with arms
3. Land with feet simultaneously on top of the box or platform
4. Land with full-foot contact and give at the knees and hips – use arms for balance and control
5. Feet should land softly on box; step back down (not jump back down) and repeat; allow 1:10 recovery ratio
6. Maintain good body posture at all times when jumping and landing as quality of movement is paramount over quantity

THE BODY COACH

69. STEP FROM BOX

| Start | Step Off | Land |

INSTRUCTION
1. Start by standing on box with both feet together, arms by side
2. Step forwards off box both with one leg
3. Land with full-foot contact of both feet and give at the knees and hips to absorb any shock
4. Use arms for balance and control
5. Maintain good body posture at all times when jumping and landing as quality of movement

Note
Exercise for advanced athletes only under direct supervision

70. DEPTH JUMP

| Start | Land | React |

INSTRUCTION

1. Start on top of box platform in a half-squat position with arms bent by side
2. Step off from the raised box platform to the ground
3. As the flight of the drop occurs, prepare for landing by flexing at the knees, hips and ankles and bringing the elbows back
4. Lower body by bending the knees and then explode upwards, extending the hips, knees, and ankles and land up on top of box with both feet
5. Upon landing, initiate a rapid jumping phase by thrusting the arms upward and extending the body for as much height as possible – keeping ground-contact (foot) time to a minimum
6. Upon landing absorb shock by bending the knees and lowering the arms for balance
7. Maintain good body posture at all times when jumping and landing as quality of movement is paramount over quantity

Note
Exercise for advanced athletes only under direct supervision

THE BODY COACH

71. DEPTH JUMP WITH SPRINT

| Start | Step Off Box | Explode Up | Land and Sprint |

INSTRUCTION

1. Start on top of box platform in a half-squat position, arms bent by side
2. Step off from the raised box to the ground
3. Upon landing, initiate a rapid jumping phase (see Exercise 70)
4. As the flight of the drop occurs, prepare for landing in sprint position by flexing at the knees, hips and ankles and bringing the elbows back
5. Upon landing, initiate sprint forwards for 10–20 meters
6. Maintain good body posture at all times when jumping and landing as quality of movement is paramount over quantity

Note

Exercise for advanced athletes only under direct supervision

Chapter 7

Speed, Power and Reaction Time

This chapter outlines drills for speed, power and reaction time performed in a sprinting environment. Which energy system is used to supply energy for muscular contraction is primarily determined by the intensity of exercise and the duration of exercise. In general, short high-intensity explosive activities rely on the phosphagen energy system with activities up to 6 seconds in duration at maximal speed.

72. FALLING STARTS

Raise onto Toes and Lean Forward　　　**React, Land and Sprint Forwards**

INSTRUCTION
1. Stand tall with feet together and hands by your side
2. Lean forward and raise up onto toes until balance is lost
3. React with two quick steps and a rapid arm drive followed by a short sprint over 20 m
4. Look forward with chest held tall and head in neutral position
5. Lean and react with arm drive and two quick steps
6. Maintain strong core and upright posture
7. Continue good body mechanics for short sprint

Variation
1. After two steps and a short sprint add change of direction – left or right
2. Add decision after short sprint – ie. dodge, weave or step
3. START and STOP – falling start, sprint 10 m and stop; repeat 4 times

73. RUNNING STARTS

(a) Sprint Start
(b) Standing Start
(c) 3-Point Start

a(i). Sprint Start – On Your Marks

a(ii). Set and Go on Call

b. Standing Start

c. 3-Point Start

Emphasis
- Develop explosive reaction from various starting positions

INSTRUCTION

(a) Sprint Start
1. Stand one foot behind line in a forward lunge position
2. Lower rear knee to ground in line with the front foot
3. Lean forwards and place hands on the line shoulder-width apart – thumbs inwards, fingers pointing out with slight arch between index finger and thumb
4. On 'set' call, raise hips into air, straighten arms, lean head over hands and up onto back toes
5. On 'GO' – explode from line and sprint forwards up to 6 seconds

(b) Standing Start
1. Stand with favored foot behind the line and other leg back resting on toes
2. Arms positioned in ready position
3. On 'GO' – explode from line and sprint forwards up to 6 seconds

(c) 3-Point Start
1. Start in sprint start position
2. Raise up into set position and extend arm of forward leg back and up off the ground
3. On 'set' call, raise hips into air, straighten arms, lean head over hands and up onto back toes
4. On 'GO' – explode from the line and sprint forwards up to 6 seconds

Teaching Points
- Relax and breathe deeply
- Focus on body position and starting call
- React as quickly as possible with explosive leg and arm drive
- Maintain square hips
- Strengthen core muscles to ensure strong torso
- Continue good body mechanics for short sprint

74. POWER BLOCK STARTS

Set   Explode

INSTRUCTION

1. Place blocks 1 foot length behind line
2. Put both hands behind line, shoulder-width apart
3. Place both feet into blocks leading with dominant leg
4. Lower rear knee to ground in line with the front foot
5. On 'your marks' call, lean forwards and place hands on the line shoulder-width apart – thumbs inwards, fingers pointing out with slight arch between index finger and thumb
6. On 'set' call, raise hips into air, straighten arms, lean head over hands and up onto back toes
7. On 'GO' – explode from the line and sprint forwards up to 6 seconds

THE BODY COACH

75. SPRINTING

Explode   **Sprint Forwards**

INSTRUCTION

1. Sprint drills are designed to improve body posture, hip position, leg and arm action, improve rate of hip extension and speed of limb recovery after push off
2. The length of your running stride affects how much distance you gain with each stride take
3. If a person can improve their **stride length** by just a few centimeters and maintain their **stride frequency**, the individual will improve speed
4. For example, more distance is gained in the same number of steps (or frequency), which in turn, means that the individual will cover more ground faster than with the shorter stride length
5. Learning basic running technique therefore provides the foundation for this to occur and should be practiced regularly all year round
6. For power focus on sprints up to 6 seconds or 60 meters in distance

Chapter 8

Upper Body Power Training

It is believed that the stretch shortening cycle (SSC) can be activated in the upper body just as it is in the lower body. The most common method of upper body plyometrics is with a medicine ball. Prior to performing upper body power drills, ensure a good core-strength base is acquired – with the ability to perform the following movements continuously and without loss of form using ones own body weight:

- 30 push-ups
- 10 wide-grip chin-ups
- 50 abdominal crunches

Note: For additional exercises see The Body Coach® Medicine Ball Basics book

76. PLYOMETRIC PUSH-UP

Kneeling

Descend, Land Absorb

INSTRUCTION (advanced athletes only)
1. Kneel on ground with hands raised in front of chest
2. Brace abdominal muscles and keep posture strong to avoid arching of the lower back
3. Lean forward and drop to the ground keeping knees bent
4. Absorb forces through eccentric loading
5. Rapidly push back up concentrically to starting position
6. Maintain good body posture at all times as quality of movement is paramount over quantity.

VARIATION
- Eccentric drop and absorb only
- Partner holds shoulders and then releases athlete forwards

77. MEDICINE BALL POWER PUSH-UPS

| Start | Push-off | Land | Explode Back onto Ba |

INSTRUCTION

1. Begin in push-up position with hands on medicine ball with fingers facing down and thumbs forward
2. Brace abdominal muscles and keep posture strong to avoid arching of the lower back
3. Quickly remove hands from the medicine ball and drop down
4. Contact the ground with both hands on either side of medicine ball wider than shoulder-width apart
5. Immediately react and push up by extending the elbows, placing hands back on top of the medicine ball
6. Repeat action for set amount of repetitions
7. Maintain good body posture at all times as quality of movement is paramount over quantity

Variation: Practice on knees to improve strength

78. MEDICINE BALL POWER CROSS

| Start | Midpoint Crossover | Endpoint |

INSTRUCTION

1. Begin in push-up position with one hand on medicine ball and elbows bent
2. Brace abdominal muscles and keep posture strong to avoid arching of the lower back
3. Explode up and across by extending the elbows
4. Switch hands on the ball and take opposite hand out to the side once again into a push-up position
5. Quickly remove hands from the medicine ball and drop down
6. Immediately react and repeat action across to opposite side again for a set amount of repetitions
7. Maintain good body posture at all times as quality of movement is paramount over quantity

Variation: Practice on knees to improve strength

79. MEDICINE BALL OVERHEAD THRUST

Start **Overhead Thrust**

INSTRUCTION

1. Stand with feet slightly wider than hip-width apart on an open field
2. Have a partner stand approximately 10-20 meters behind you to trap ball after first or second bounce, upon landing
3. Grasp ball and lower body into a semi-squat position
4. Explode upwards off the ground using the legs whilst simultaneously thrusting medicine ball up and over the head
5. Land properly by bending at the knees and hips to absorb shock
6. The aim is to throw the ball behind you as far as possible – generating most of the power in the legs
7. Repeat drill according to prescribed repetitions

THE BODY COACH

80. MEDICINE BALL POWER THROW DOWNS

| Start | Throw Down |

INSTRUCTION

1. Stand with feet parallel and knees slightly bent
2. Holding medicine ball in hands, extend arms above head
3. Brace abdominal muscles and keep posture strong to avoid arching of the lower back
4. Simultaneously jump up as you forcefully thrust medicine ball down in front of body to the ground
5. Land in control by bending the knees to absorb the shock and catch the ball on the first bounce
6. Repeat drill according to prescribed repetitions

81. MEDICINE BALL ABDOMINAL THRUSTS

Start

Thrust Forwards

INSTRUCTION

1. Sit on ground with legs slightly bent and arms in front of body
2. A partner standing 2–5 meters away passes a medicine ball at the athletes' chest
3. The athlete catches the ball, bracing the stomach – allowing the force to push the upper body back and down to the ground with the medicine ball; extending arms overhead
4. The athlete then immediately sitsup thrusting the ball overhead back to the partner
5. Repeat movement according to prescribed repetitions
6. Maintain good body posture at all times as quality of movement is paramount over quantity

Note: This exercise can be performed as a chest pass also from the ground

THE BODY COACH

82. MEDICINE BALL ROTARY THRUST

| Start | Thrust Across |

INSTRUCTION

1. Stand with feet hip-width apart
2. Hold medicine ball with both hands and arms only slightly bent
3. Swing ball over to the left hip and forcefully underhand toss ball across body to a partner (wall or open field)
4. Keep the stomach drawn in to maximize proper usage of muscle
5. Catch ball on the bounce from your partner or wall and repeat according to prescribed repetitions
6. Maintain good body posture at all times as quality of movement is paramount over quantity
7. Rest and repeat drill from right side

83. MEDICINE BALL TRICEPS THRUST

| Start | Thrust Forwards |

INSTRUCTION

1. Ensure clear open space is available
2. Stand with feet together and medicine ball overhead
3. Hold medicine ball with both hands and arms only slightly bent
4. Brace abdominal muscles and keep posture strong to avoid arching of the lower back
5. Simultaneously step forwards and extend arms rapidly releasing the medicine ball across an open area
6. Land in lunge position and walk or jog forwards to retrieve medicine ball
7. Maintain good body posture at all times as quality of movement is paramount over quantity

VARIATION

- Triceps thrust to partner – allow ball to bounce before catching
- Thrust against solid concrete wall 5–10 meters away – allow ball to bounce before catching

THE BODY COACH

Chapter 9

Power
Training
Routines

Power plyometrics are a form of progressive resistance exercise and thus, must follow the principles of progressive overload. Progressive overload is a systematic increase in frequency, volume and intensity by various combinations of exercises. Keep in mind that when one or two of these variables are increased, one or both of the other variables may decrease. Generally, as intensity increases volume will decrease.

A typical plyometric program will take place over 8 weeks with two training sessions per week. The method of progressive overload is dependent upon the sport and training phase. An off-season plyometric program for sport, for example, may be performed two times a week. The program would progress in two week phases:

1. Low to moderate volume of low-intensity
2. Low to moderate volumes and medium intensity
3. Low to moderate volumes of high intensity

This example could serve for any sport, with differing exercises utilizing the same progression of intensity and volume. Proper progression into a plyometric program as well as within the program includes:

- Athlete evaluation
- Goals and length of program established
- Proper techniques have been demonstrated, practiced and learnt
- Athletes understand focus and attention to detail with all exercises
- Quality of movement in a fresh state is paramount
- Proper warm-up and cooldown is part of power training
- Drills progress from low to high intensity
- Drills progress from low to high volume
- Motor skills are continually being developed, assessed and improved

Designing Program

The total numbers of sets, repetitions, and rest intervals (recovery) is dependant on a number of factors. Frequency, volume, intensity, progression, and recovery all refer to the training session itself.

Factors	Guidelines
Frequency is the number of workouts per week.	• One to two times per week due to the high intensity nature of such workouts • 48-72 hours between sessions
Volume relates to the number of repetitions per session. For lower body exercises a repetition is a ground contact.	• Low volume 60–80 foot contacts • Moderate 80–150 foot contacts • High volume is 150–300 foot contacts
Intensity refers to the amount of stress placed on the muscle during the workout.	• Start with low intensity stationary jumps and hops on both legs and master these before progressing to single leg drills and multiple jumps or hops, directional changes and speed of movement.
Progression is the change from low-intensity to medium-intensity to high-intensity levels as the athlete progresses.	• Progress through the stress continuum of low to medium to high intensity.
Recovery is the rest that is allowed between the individual sets of the drills. • The effectiveness of a plyometric training session depends on maximal effort and a high speed of movement for each repetition. Rest intervals between repetitions and sets should be long enough to allow almost complete recovery. Plyometric drills should not be performed when an athlete is fatigued. Rest between sets must ensure complete recovery.	• 2-3 minutes between sets of low to moderate level • 3 minutes at high intensity between sets with up to 15 seconds rest between each rep involving shock drills • As much as 5-10 seconds may be required between various jumps and a work to rest ratio of 1:10 is recommended. • 48-72 hours between sessions
Repetition (rep) is the single, complete action of an exercise.	• Utilize volume and athlete skill level to determine the number of reps. These are generally broken down into approximately 10 repetitions.
Sets consists of a given number of complete and continuous repetitions of an exercise.	• Work between 1-3 sets, over 8 weeks before increasing.

Stress Continuum Chart

The following table is designed to show examples of low, medium and high intensity drills. Remember, this is only a blueprint and should be modified based on the sport, period of season and the athlete's level of ability.

	Low Intensity	Medium Intensity	High Intensity
Stationary Jumps	Squat Jump	Double Leg Tuck Jump	Double Leg Vertical Power Jump
Standing Jumps	–	Standing Long Jump	Standing Triple Jump
Short-response Hops	Two Ankle Foot Hop	Double Leg Hop	Single Leg Hop
Long-Response Hops	Single Leg Hops	Alternate Leg Bound	Double Leg Speed Hop
Bounds	Bounds	Alternate Leg Bound	Alternate Leg Diagonal Bound
Upper Body Plyometrics	Medicine Ball Abdominal Thrust	Medicine Ball Push-up	Overhead Backward Throw

Low Intensity Plyometric Workout – Stationary

- 3 exercises
- 2 sets of 10 repetitions
- 60 contacts

Exercises

Squat Jump	Medicine Ball Abdominal Thrust	Split Squat Jump

2 sets of 10 Reps	2 sets of 10 Reps	2 sets of 10 Reps
Rest 2 minutes	Rest 2 minutes	Rest 2 minutes
Page: 33	Page: 118	Page: 43

PLYOMETRICS RECORD SHEET

EXERCISE	REPS	SETS	REST
Squat Jump	10	2	2 mins
Medicine Ball Abdominal Thrust	10	2	2 mins
Split Squat Jump	10	2	2 mins

Medium Intensity Plyometric Workout – Stationary

- 3 exercises
- 2 sets of 10 repetitions
- 60 contacts

Exercises

Straight Pike Jump	Medicine Ball Power Push-ups	Double Leg Tuck Jump

2 sets of 10 Reps Rest 2 minutes Page: 46	2 sets of 10 Reps Rest 2 minutes Page: 114	2 sets of 10 Reps Rest 2 minutes Page: 38

PLYOMETRICS RECORD SHEET

EXERCISE	REPS	SETS	REST
Pike Jump	10	2	2 mins
Medicine Ball Power Push-ups	10	2	2 mins
Double Leg Tuck Jump	10	2	2 mins

High Intensity Plyometric Workout – Stationary

- 3 exercises
- 2 sets of 10 repetitions
- 60 contacts

Exercises

Split Pike Jump	Medicine Ball Overhead Thrust	Scissors Jump

2 sets of 10 Reps Rest 3 minutes Page: 45	2 sets of 10 Reps Rest 3 minutes Page: 116	2 sets of 8-10 Reps Rest 3 minutes Page: 40

PLYOMETRICS RECORD SHEET

EXERCISE	REPS	SETS	REST
Split Pike Jump	10	2	3 mins
Overhead Medicine Ball Thrust	10	2	3 mins
Scissor Jump	8-10	2	3 mins

Short Response and Long Response Hops

Hops and bounds can be either long or short response. Short response bounds are performed quickly, one after the other. Long response bounds are performed in the same fashion as short response bounds. The difference is noted in the loading time between jumps. Long response jumps allow for more controlled eccentric loading between jumps.

Exercises

| Double Leg Zig-Zag Hop | Double Leg Hops | Single Leg Hops |

2 sets of hops over 20 meters
Rest 3 minutes
Page: 81

2 sets of hops over 20 meters
Rest 3 minutes
Page: 84

1 set of 10 hops each leg over 20 meters
Rest 3 minutes
Page: 89

PLYOMETRICS RECORD SHEET

EXERCISE	REPS	SETS	REST
Double Leg Zig-Zag Hop	10	2	3 mins
Double Leg Hop	10	2	3 mins
Single Leg Hop	10	1 each leg	3 mins

THE BODY COACH

Sample Sports Plyometric Training Sessions

Below are sample plyometric training sessions for badminton and tennis, basketball and volleyball, rugby and soccer.

Badminton and Tennis

Exercises	Sets and Repetitions
Split Squat Jumps	2 x 10
Medicine Ball Triceps Thrusts	2 x 10
Multiple Box Jumps	2 x 10
Medicine Ball Rotary Thrusts	2 x 10 each side

Basketball and Volleyball

Exercises	Sets and Repetitions
Depth Jumps	2 x 8
Medicine Ball Abdominal Thrusts	2 x 10
Missile Jumps	2 x 10
Multiple Box Jumps	2 x 10

Rugby

Exercises	Sets and Repetitions
Zig-Zag Hops	4 x 8
Rotary Thrusts	2 x 8 each side
Medicine Ball Power Cross	2 x 10
Medicine Ball Overhead Throws	2 x 10

Soccer

Exercises	Sets and Repetitions
Split Jump	2 x 10
Medicine Ball Abdominal Thrusts	2 x 8 each side
Zig-Zag Hops	4 x 8
Power Block Starts	1 x 10

THE BODY COACH™
www.thebodycoach.com

International Managing Agent

Saxton Speakers Bureau (Australia)
- Website: www.saxton.com.au
- Email: speakers@saxton.com.au
- Phone: (03) 9811 3500
  International: +61 3 9811 3500

www.thebodycoach.com

Study in Australia

- International Fitness College for overseas students to study sport, fitness and personal training qualifications in Sydney Australia
- 3 month to 2 year student visa courses

www.sportandfitness.com.au

AUSTRALIAN ACADEMY OF SPORT AND FITNESS

Power Training Index

The Body Coach

Paul Collins
Fitness Ball Drills

Fitness Ball Drills is a user-friendly exercise guide for achieving a stronger, leaner and more flexible body. The Fitness Ball is one of the most utilized pieces of gym and fitness equipment used throughout the world to tone, stretch and strengthen the whole body. Body Coach Paul Collins provides step-by-step coaching for improving posture, balance, coordination, strength and flexibility with more than 50 exercises that can easiliy be carried out at home or in the gym. Fitness Ball Drills is the perfect book for those who seek to improve their total body fitness.

144 pages, full-color print
182 color photos
Paperback, 6¹/₂" x 9¹/₄"
ISBN: 978-1-84126-221-5
$ 14.95 US/$ 20.95 CDN
£ 9.95 UK/€ 14.95

The Body Coach

Paul Collins
Stretching Basics

Stretching Basics is a user-friendly exercise guide for achieving a more supple and flexible body using your own body as resistance. It provides an introductory guide for stretching and flexibility exercises for sport, lifestyle, and injury prevention. Body Coach Paul Collins provides step-by-step instructions for more then 50 exercises meant to improve flexibility and range of motion, as well as to reduce muscular tension throughout the whole body. Stretching Basics is ideal for all age groups and ability levels.

144 pages, full-color print
255 color photos
Paperback, 6^1/2" x 9^1/4"
ISBN: 978-1-84126-220-8
$ 14.95 US/$ 20.95 CDN
£ 9.95 UK/€ 14.95

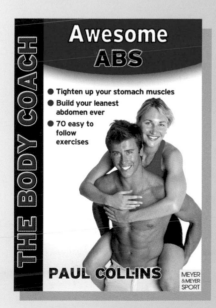

Paul Collins
Awesome Abs

The abdominal muscles serve a critical function in daily movement, sport and physical activity. A strong midsection helps support and protect your lower back region from injury. Awesome Abs is packed with over 70 easy-to-follow exercises and tests aimed at achieving a leaner abdomen, a stronger lower back, better posture and a trimmer waistline. You'll not only look and feel better, but athletes will find that a well-conditioned midsection allows them to change direction faster, generate force quicker and absorb blows better.

144 pages, full-color print
200 photos & illustrations
Paperback, 6^1/2" x 9^1/4"
ISBN: 978-1-84126-232-1
$14.95 US / $19.95 CDN
£ 9.95 UK/€ 14.95

Photo & Illustration Credits